Zen Philosophy

ZEN PHILOSOPHY

A PRACTICAL GUIDE TO HAPPINESS AND PEACE

NATHAN BELLOW

Copyright © 2014 by Nathan Bellow

Zen Philosophy

WHY YOU SHOULD READ THIS BOOK

Zen philosophy is a concept that has enriched and fueled peoples lives for centuries. The proponents of the philosophy have let go of materialistic endeavors, simplified their lives, fueled themselves toward their true passions, and enriched their relationships with their friends and family members.

In this racing, schedule-oriented lifestyle, it's difficult to find your true voice and your true purpose. This is natural. The stress hormone cortisol is a constant opponent against your natural calm ways, and you find yourself bug-eyed, wandering around lost in this monstrous rat race.

You don't have to be in the rat race anymore. Take yourself out of your schedule for just a few minutes every day, and orient yourself in Zen meditation. It's an ancient tradition: one that benefits your interior mind and fuels you with the power to move forward. You can close your mind from your racing thoughts. They don't have to follow you wherever you go. In fact, you can strip them off like a sweater and fall into the actual reality of yourself: yourself beyond your racing thoughts, beyond your brimming schedule. You can find out what truly makes you unique.

Zen Philosophy

Zen philosophy makes people happier than they've been before. It allows them to find meaningful connections in this harried world, and it allows them to rev toward their true goals, their true missions. With Zen meditation, outlined for you in step-by-step instructions in this book, you can begin the process of getting back to yourself. You can finally lend yourself the necessary relief you require to maximize your life and your internal goals.

Achieve greater happiness. Reap the rewards of this ancient Indian, Chinese, and Japanese tradition. Find inner peace, and help your fellow man. Eliminate your stressors and reduce your chance of depression. You can live the life you've always wanted by stepping away from yourself for just thirty minutes a day. Allow this Zen teaching to be your guide.

Zen Philosophy

ABOUT THE AUTHOR

My mission with this is to be able to help inspire and change the world, one reader at a time.

I want to provide the most amazing life tools that anyone can apply into their lives. It doesn't matter whether you have hit rock bottom in your life or your life is amazing and you want to keep taking it to another level.

If you are like me, then you are probably looking to become the best version of yourself. You are likely not to settle for an okay life. You want to live an extraordinary life. Not only to be filled within but also to contribute to society.

Zen Philosophy

ALL RIGHTS RESERVED. This book contains material protected under International and Federal Copyright Laws and Treaties. Any unauthorized reprint or use of this material is prohibited. No part of this book may be reproduced or transmitted in any form or by any means, electronic or mechanical, including photocopying, recording, or by any information storage and retrieval system without express written permission from the author / publisher.

Any unauthorized broadcasting; public performance, copying or re-recording will constitute an infringement of copyright.

Permission granted to reproduce for personal and educational use only. Commercial copying, hiring, lending is prohibited.

May be used free of charge. Selling without prior written consent prohibited. Obtain permission before redistributing. In all cases this notice must remain intact.

Zen Philosophy

TABLE OF CONTENTS

CHAPTER 1. ZEN PHILOSOPHY: AN INTRODUCTION

CHAPTER 2. THE HISTORY OF ZEN PHILOSOPHY

CHAPTER 3. BENEFITS OF ZEN BUDDHISM

CHAPTER 4. HOW TO PRACTICE ZEN MEDITATION

CHAPTER 5. A GUIDE TO GREATER ZEN HAPPINESS

CHAPTER 6. ACHIEVE ENLIGHTENMENT: A LOOK TOWARD A ZEN FUTURE

ABOUT THE AUTHOR

OTHER BOOKS BY : NATHAN BELLOW

Chapter 1. Zen Philosophy: An Introduction

Zen is an element of Mahayana Buddhism, a meditative, spiritual process first created in India thousands of years ago. Zen brings emphasis to the practice of meditation in order to achieve ultimate awakening and enlightenment. After Zen's initial creation, it spread like fire to China, Vietnam, Japan, Korea, and finally to the rest of the world.

The actual word "Zen" comes from a Middle Chinese word and its subsequent Japanese pronunciation. The word is a derivation of the word dhyana, which you might know if you've studied the initial history of yoga and meditation. The actual word, dhyana, means a meditative state.

The emphasis of the idea of Zen lends insight to the Buddha and interior personal understanding of one's self. It further emphasizes understanding one's everyday life and how to fuel one's everyday life to benefit one's peers. Therefore, unlike many other "enlightened" ideas, Zen does not fuel only the literature of the Zen doctrine or Zen sutras. It looks to life comprehension through communication with a Zen Buddhist teacher and an idea called zazen.

Introduction to Zazen

Zen Philosophy

Zazen literally means "seated meditation" and is a well-known meditative discipline. It varies from different Zen traditions; however, it is essentially a way to understand the reasons one exists in this world: "The meaning of life." Zazen lies at the very heart of Zen Buddhism and therefore becomes incredibly important in daily practice. When one incorporates zazen, one begins to suspend judgmental thoughts, allow words and ideas to flow freely, and sit solemnly and quietly.

Zazen Methods

1. Sitting.

Zazen in Zen temples allows practitioners to simply sit in zazen in a group. This usually occurs in a meditation hall, called a zendo. Each of the meditation practitioners sit on a zafu, or a particular cushion, which is further boosted atop a flat, low-to-the ground mat, also known as a zabuton.

Prior to sitting atop the cushion, the meditation practitioner always bows a particular gassho bow to the cushion. He further bows to his other practitioners.

The zazen period is kick started by three rings of a bell. The end of the zazen is initiated by ringing the bell either one time or two times. If the seated zazen ceremony lasts a long time, the practitioners might initiate intervals of walking meditation called kinhin.

Zen Philosophy

2. POSTURE.

The zazen requires a particular posture. The practitioner sits with both folded hands and legs. His spine is high, sturdy, but settled. Both of his hands are folded over the stomach. The practitioner works to breathe from the very center of his gravity, otherwise called the hara. Furthermore, his eyes are only half-open so that the eyes are not completely distracted by the exterior world nor eliminating the stimuli from complete comprehension.

The various leg posture styles are:

Hankafuza
Kekkafuza
Seiza
Burmese

In this case, Kekkafuza is the full-lotus position; Hankafuza is the half-lotus position; Burmese is the cross-legged, ankles together in the front position; and Seiza is a posture that revolves around kneeling with the occasional utilization of a bench.

In the general sense, Zazen has three teachings: Concentration, Koan, and Shikantaza.

CONCENTRATION:

The first stages of the traditional teachings of zazen

Zen Philosophy

emphasize ultimate concentration. You are meant to focus your breath directly on the hara, and the mind is meant to be continually counting to eight, over and over. This form of counting meditation is also called susokukan. Some zazen practitioners utilize a mantra along with the breathing practices. This practice is continued over and over until the practitioner works to experience something called "Samadhi." This is a oneness, or the central theme of one's mind. After the practitioner reaches this Samadhi, he can move forward with the following zazen methods.

KOAN INTROSPECTION:

After the practitioner of zazen has developed ultimate concentration and awareness in the previous step, the practitioner can turn his thoughts towards koans. Koans are not easily solvable in their nature. Therefore, turning one's concentration towards koans actually turns the mind to the reality that exists in the realms beyond thoughts. More on this idea later.

Shikantaza:

Shikantaza is the next form of the zazen in which the person utilizing zazen does not require an object to meditate toward. Instead, practitioners attempt to exist completely in the present. They are ultimately aware of what's happening both around them and in their interior minds. It is the art of "no thoughts."

Various Zen teachings encompass Mahayana thought,

Zen Philosophy

including the Tathagatagarbha Sutras, the Yogacara, and the Huayan.

Zen Philosophy

Chapter 2. The History of Zen Philosophy

Zen: Rooted in Indian Practices

The Zen philosophy dates back thousands of years ago, to Buddha's lifetime in India. Buddha was born near the border of Nepal and India in the year 563 BC. When he was born, his initial identity was Prince Siddhartha Guatama. When he was twenty-nine years old, Siddhartha left his home and changed history forever.

At that time, Yoga was Siddharth's practice to concentrate his interior spirit toward one pivotal point: this point was an achievement of ultimate feelings of serenity through zazen, or seated meditation. Yoga methods of these initial Indian days looked to food and drink restrictions, fasts, and vows. Many people, for example, take the vow to remain standing on one particular leg for a long period of time. When the training yogi worked himself through these various tests, he was meant to train himself into a feeling of indifference to the world's stimuli. Because his body and its needs were also stimuli, he had to train himself to forget about them. He was meant to control every movement in his soul.

According to tradition, Buddha himself utilized this yoga for over ten years, after he renounced the duties of his former mundane existence and began to travel. He traveled to four corners of India in order to interview

Zen Philosophy

both saints and wise men. During his interviews, he was unable to find essential answers to his ultimate questions:

1. What is man?

2. How should man live?

After he had traveled for so long, searching for the answers to his questions, he sat down. He crossed both his legs, supposedly under the Bodhi tree, and he studied his breathing. He inhaled and exhaled and attempted to remove himself from his surrounding world. When he did this for forty-nine days, he finally achieved this higher level of feeling, of consciousness. He was able to see the light of a star. Afterwards, he understood his actual universal nature. He grew to understand the existence of every man, woman, and child, and he became the Buddha.

ZEN GROWTH IN CHINA

Zen was proffered to Chinese individuals by a man named Boddhidharma. Boddhidharma was the representation of the twenty-eighth generation of the original Buddha discipline. He had learned the Buddha discipline after several generations of teachers and students, after a timespan lasting a few hundred years.

When Boddhidharma arrived to China, the country was divided, in war. There was a constant struggle for power

Zen Philosophy

in each of the states, and chaos was absolute. The Liang dynasty was the ruler of one of these ancient Chinese states, and its emperor, Wu-Ti, invited Boddhidharma to his palace. Wu-Ti was a pupil of Buddhism.

The emperor, Wu-Ti, asked Boddhidharma this question: "What is the basic principle of Buddhism." Boddhidharma answered: "An immense vacuum. A clear sky. A sky which does not distinguish between the enlightened and the ignorant. The world exactly as it is."

Wu-Ti could not comprehend this message. Therefore, Boddhidharma declared that Zen was not ready to come to China. He left Wu-Ti's state, and he crossed over the Yang-Tse river. He retired in the Northern Mountains, in a Shorin temple, in which he could practice zazen by a wall for a full nine years.

Six generations after Boddhidharma attempted to bring Zen to China, Zen spread like wild fire via the Zen master, Eno. When Eno entered China, his teachings allowed Zen to spread into five different schools of Zen: Igyo, Hongen, Soto, Unmon, and Rinzai. Thousands of Chinese temples were formed in the forests and the mountains, and a subsequent huge Buddhist population formed around the temples. Zen became the quintessential part of the Chinese civilization. Note: only three of these subsections of Chinese schools reached Japan. These were Soto, Rinzai, and Obaku.

ZEN GROWTH IN JAPAN

Zen Philosophy

The Rinzai Zen Buddhism and the Soto Zen Buddhism took their roots in Japan. Rinzai Buddhist tradition was based on the strict discipline that participants utilize to disarticulate their mental thoughts. The Koan focus, mentioned previously, became the essential aspect of the Rinzai tradition. According to tradition, when one utilizes Koan, one can reach beyond the realms of one's thoughts and intelligence. One can find immediate awakening.

The Soto tradition, also oriented in Japan, places ultimate concentration on Buddha's life. Therefore, one is meant to follow Buddha's daily tradition and advance his daily practice. One is not meant to expect exceptional things from one's life. Instead, he is meant to sit. And exist.

Zen Buddhism effects many-a-daily life of the Japanese people. One can view the difference in all Japanese culture: from eating to painting, clothing to calligraphy, theater to music, gardening to decorating, etc. Although many Japanese people do not practice Zen Buddhism today, Zen Buddhism remains a part of their culture and therefore a part of them. The influence of its teachings is rich in the souls of all the Japanese people.

Zen Growth in the United States

Zen Buddhism came to the western world in 1893, when a man named Soyen Shaku came to the World Parliament of Religions, held that year in Chicago. More than ten years later, Soyen Shaku came back to the United States and taught Zen Buddhism in San Francisco. From there,

15

Zen Philosophy

Zen Buddhist teachings churned in California. Eventually, the idea of Buddhism was popularized by Jack Kerouac's 1957 novel, *The Dharma Bums*. According to Time magazine, "Zen Buddhism [was] growing more chic by the minute."

Today, Buddhism is one of the most popular religions in the United States, equal in size to Hinduism and Islam and behind Christianity, non-religion, and Judaism.

Zen Philosophy

CHAPTER 3. BENEFITS OF ZEN BUDDHISM

Zen meditation practice links the observation of your mind with the observation of your body, yielding a sense of "otherness" beyond reality. It is different than other forms of meditation, which is generally practiced to initiate stress relief or find interior relaxation. However, Zen meditation is utilized to get to the root of deep interior anxieties and problems. It is meant to initiate an understanding between you and your core of pain and fear. To connect to a greater peace of mind and a deeper sense of tranquility, look to the following essential benefits of the Zen meditation.

1. REDUCE ANXIETY AND STRESS

Deep life stressors and feelings of anxiety are natural parts of one's life. However, you don't have to let them walk all over you and rule your interior being. When these feelings overtake you, you can lose track of yourself, of your motivation to live, and of your relationships with people. With Zen meditation practices, you can completely empty your mind from these stressors. You can replace these stressed feelings with the knowledge of the truth of your existence. This knowledge is a sort of freedom, an initiation into an "otherness" that has nothing to do with all of the things you have to do tomorrow. You can relinquish yourself from your packed schedule. You can find internal peace.

Zen Philosophy

2. Fuel Feelings of Interior Clarity

Living with a packed schedule is a natural part of most people's existence. As a culture, we are constantly going and going, and we don't often take a chance to stop, smell the flowers, and clear our minds. When you practice Zen meditation, however, you learn to find clarity in your thoughts. With these clear, defined thoughts, you can make sure, impactful choices. You can limit your intrusive, uninformed thoughts during your meditation practices, therefore allowing yourself to empty your mind even further. The point of Zen meditation is to move forward from your thoughts to a place beyond reality. In this place, you must have complete clarity to define your existence.

3. Stave Off Chronic Depression

Every year, thousands and thousands of people are diagnosed with depression. This depression is a result of our lifestyle choices, of our packed schedules, and of our eating habits. So often, these diagnoses are answered with synthetic antidepressants that alter brain chemistry and have other unfortunate side effects. Furthermore, many people become dependent on these synthetic drugs and cannot function without them. Because depression is the ultimate result of stress and anxiety, deep Zen meditation and interior focus can allow you to understand the reasons behind your depression. You can begin to find the root of your problem with depression

Zen Philosophy

instead of simply treating the symptoms. Isn't it better to stop the reserve of depressive power at its internal source?

4. CREATE A BETTER SLEEP CYCLE

When you find better clarity in your thoughts and begin to reduce your anxiety and depression, you can create a better sleep schedule. This, in turn, orients you down the path of handling your stress and anxiety much better. After all, poor sleep creates anxiety, stress, and depression. A lack of depression, stress, and anxiety creates a better sleep schedule. It's cyclical. Furthermore, meditation reveals an interior awareness of yourself, creating understanding of yourself that you might not have had before. When you create a better interior understanding, you don't have as many questions about yourself and your purpose in the minutes—or hours—before you go to sleep. You don't have to ponder the point of your life. You already understand it, on an intimate level, and you can allow your consciousness to simply fall away. Also, meditation lends you feelings of deep internal happiness, which is essential for better rest.

5. HOLD BETTER SELF-CONFIDENCE AND GREATER INNER TRUST

When you hone your mind with Zen meditation, you can create more focused and clear decisions. With these clear

Zen Philosophy

decisions comes a better feeling of self-confidence and trust in your abilities. You can take on more responsibilities because you trust yourself to do well with those responsibilities. Furthermore, when you begin to learn more about yourself on an interior level, understanding yourself and your interior mission, you can reach toward a greater self-confidence because you understand that each action you take has a greater purpose.

6. FORMULATE STRONGER RELATIONSHIP BONDS

Zen meditation boosts your interior understanding of yourself, your thoughts, and how you relate to those thoughts. This is key in order to better your personal relationships. Because you already understand how you operate via your actions on a very intimate level, you can decipher why other people act the way they do via their internal thoughts and actions. Perhaps before you practiced Zen meditation, you couldn't truly stand in another person's shoes, so to speak, to really reach to how they felt about something. When you practice Zen meditation, you not only hold better understanding for yourself; you can reach toward other people with more compassion and empathy. Also, you can communicate with these people more precisely because you have better clarity of thoughts. Have you ever had an argument in which you felt like the idea you're trying to translate isn't coming through to your friend or family member? This imperfect interaction simply won't occur

Zen Philosophy

anymore when you transition your life to incorporate Zen meditation.

7. STRENGTHEN YOUR FAITH, REGARDLESS OF YOUR BELIEFS

Regardless of your religious beliefs, Zen meditation allows you to formulate a better dialogue with yourself and with any higher power. This is because Zen meditation is incredibly deep, aligning thoughts, breathing, posture, and counting to push you toward the area beyond reality and beyond human consciousness. As you push yourself to this arena, you can allow God to speak to you. You can pray from the very core of your body, or you can meditate on a particular religious passage you've always heard but never really understood. Your meditation practices will reveal its true meaning.

Zen Philosophy

Chapter 4. How to Practice Zen Meditation

When you begin your Zen practices in order to achieve enlightenment and relinquish yourself from a dull life of material possessions and interior, racing thoughts, you must look to the following practices for maximum Zen.

Of course, as aforementioned, Zen practices appear in two formations: in zazen and in conversation with a Zen teacher. Because Zen teachers are hard to come by, it might be best to self-teach your mind to relinquish its distractions. After all, that's what Buddha did. If it was good enough for him and his ever-searching brain, it's good enough for the rest of us.

Find a Proper Environment

When you're looking to practice zazen, you must find your proper environment in which to meditate. This environment must be quiet: a place free from a wind or any smoke. This place shouldn't be in your kitchen, for example, because you might feel the distractions from your cupboard and your refrigerator calling out to you. You shouldn't practice in your bedroom because it's far too easy to fall into your bed and take a nap rather than honing your mind. You should find a room that's neither too bright nor too dark. The temperature should match the outdoors seasons.

Zen Philosophy

CREATE THE ZAFU AND THE ZABUTON

Zen meditation is meant to be practiced from a specific round-shaped cushion. In Japanese, this is called a zafu. The cushion is meant to raise up your hips and force your knees down to the ground. This allows your zazen to hold both stability and comfort.

When you're looking for your zafu, try to find one about fourteen inches in diameter and packed with either buckwheat or kapok. If you're a beginner and not willing to purchase a zafu yet, you can fold a large blanket into a cushion.

You'll further need a zabuton. This is a mat that you put beneath the zafu in order to cushion both your legs and your hanging knees. You can also utilize a different blanket beneath your folded blanket to create the zabuton.

PRACTICE ZEN MEDITATION

When you become a practitioner of the zazen, you can utilize up to four different types of positions. (Note: if you're a beginner, it's best if you look to the half lotus or the Burmese first before working up to the other positions.) Furthermore, remember that when you practice Zen Buddhism, the most important part of your training is to hold your neck bones and your spine in an upright position. Your posture must always be erect and strong.

Zen Philosophy

1. *Half Lotus or Hankafuza.*

As aforementioned, the half lotus is the most important starting point for your Zen Buddhism training.

Begin by sitting down in the very center of your zafu or blanket. Your butt should be centered. Next, bend up your right leg and turn it so that you see the outer side of your leg. Your right knee should be lingering atop the zabuton. Stretch your foot closely up to the zafu. Afterwards, bend up your left leg and place your left foot directly on your right thigh. Allow both of your knees to fall onto the zabuton. Your first time might be tricky to stretch this way. However, practice will allow your muscles to unfold.

2. *Full Lotus or Kekkafuza.*

The full lotus position is the standard quality position for experts of the zazen. Begin by preparing yourself in the half lotus posture. Afterwards, hold onto your right foot and bring your right leg directly overtop your left leg. Place your right foot atop of your left ghith. The legs should be criss-crossed with each of your feet resting on the opposite leg's thigh.

3. *Seiza, or Proper Sitting.*

Seiza is a classic Japanese meditation posture. When you utilize Seiza, you can breathe and expand the tanden. You

Zen Philosophy

can create a very real feeling of interior centeredness. When you maintain an image of your spine as an energetic pathway, you can create better understanding of both stillness in movement and movement in stillness, an essential part of Zen Buddhism.

Begin by kneeling to the floor and folding each of your legs beneath you. Your buttocks should rest on top of your heels. Your ankles must be turned toward your exterior, and your tops of your feet should create a small V shape. The tops of your feet should be directly on the floor. During this pose, your hands should be folded directly in your lap or, alternately, rounded up and touching the floor on either side of your cushion.

4. BURMESE.

The Burmese is an incredibly easy position, ready for any beginner. When you sit in Burmese, you must cross your legs and allow your feet to rest on the cushion directly in front of the center of your body. The knees should further stretch beyond your cushion and fall to the floor beside your cushion. As you do this, stretch your body up and forward. Imagine that the very top of your head is pushing toward the ceiling. Allow your spine to straighten, and then allow the muscles to completely relax.

5. THE HAND POSITION, OR THE HOKKAIJOIN.

When you formulate your hands in the Burmese, half lotus, and full lotus positions, you always do it the same

Zen Philosophy

way, using Hokkaijoin. Begin by placing your right hand on your left ankle with your palm to the ceiling. Your hand should be close to your stomach, and your wrist should be directly on your right thigh. Afterwards, place your left hand on your right palm with your left palm up, as well. Your left hand's fingers should cover the right hand's fingers. Allow your left wrist to sit on your left thigh, and curve your hands. Allow your thumbs to touch and create a firm line between your thumbs. Your thumbs should lightly touch right around your body's navel. Allow your shoulders to completely relax, even at their spine-stretching height. Keep your arms a bit away from the rest of your torso and waist in order to create a horizontal line from elbow to elbow.

6. PAY ATTENTION TO THE BACK AND THE NECK.

When you practice Zazen, you must keep your neck and your back erect. Allow your chin to pull back a bit, and attempt to push at the ceiling above your head with the very top of your crown. Find a sort of balance in your posture that allows you not to be too tense or too relaxed. Keep your core sort of tight so that you don't fold right, left, forward, or backward. Keep your nose tip in direct line with your body's navel.

7. PAY ATTENTION TO YOUR MOUTH AND YOUR TONGUE.

It sounds silly, but you need to pay attention to nearly every part of your body in order to learn how to forget

Zen Philosophy

about them. When you're practicing zazen, you m[...]
keep your mouth closed. You can dot your tongue to [...]
roof of your mouth, in the area just behind your teeth.
Keep your lips completely closed, and allow your teeth to
stay together. Keep your breathing in and out of your
nose.

8. PAY ATTENTION TO YOUR EYES.

When you practice zazen, you must keep your eyes in a
complete natural position to set yourself up to achieve
"none-feeling." Therefore, you must half-close your eyes
so as to relinquish yourself from total exterior
stimulation. You cannot close yourself off completely
from this exterior stimulation, and you cannot turn
yourself in completely to your interior thoughts. Allow
your eyes to focus on something about a meter directly in
front of you on the floor. Be careful that you don't close
your eyes so that you don't fall into a daze.

9. PAY ATTENTION TO YOUR BREATHING.

Breathing is an important part of Zen meditation.
Surprisingly, the traditional Zen masters never actually
taught it, proclaiming it to be easily achieved via the
correct zazen posture. When you meditate, you must
breathe slowly and quietly through your nostrils. You
must keep your mouth completely closed. Try to create a
strong, slow, even rhythm with your breathing. Allow
your body to tell you when you require more oxygen, and
allow the process to fuel itself. Don't think about it too

without noticing.

A STATE OF BEING.

...ing in zazen, your goal is to fall ...ate of non-thinking. You are meant to fall into the reality beyond thinking. Therefore, you must avoid formulating "intentional," necessary thoughts. You must avoid creating images in your head. You must allow your unconscious mind to create whatever images or thoughts it wants to. It will naturally do this, and you cannot become judgmental to these thoughts or images. Furthermore, don't pursue these thoughts and images. Simply allow them to flow through you like they're on their way to somewhere else.

Furthermore, the more fight you put up against these natural thoughts, the more strength and vitality you give to these thoughts. When you think about not thinking about them, they come at you again and again. Hold your posture firm and continue to breathe. Allow your mind to fall into tranquility, and fuel the undisturbed nature of zazen.

TO BEGIN ZAZEN

When you begin zazen, you should look toward a wall to avoid external stimuli and calm your mind. Fold your zafu overtop your zabuton about three feet from the wall. Afterwards, bring yourself into your chosen position. Breathe deeply in this position, feeling your body from

Zen Philosophy

the inside. Give yourself the appropriate hand position. Erect your back to formulate your higher posture, and begin your zazen. Practice for about twenty-five minutes your first time, and do not be discouraged if you're sore. You're a beginner. After all: it took Buddha forty-nine days of constant meditation to find enlightenment. If you can't get your mind off what you're having for dinner, you must have further training. There's always time for that.

To Finish Zazen.

After the initial twenty-five minutes have been completed and you are ready to rest from your zazen posture, you must remain calm and keep yourself low-energy for a moment. Begin by moving your legs first. Stand up slowly, and don't begin to speak right away. Allow yourself to fold out of the meditation organically, like a flower. When you find yourself ready to begin your day, you'll have the interior core of relaxation to refine the rest of your day's activities.

Understanding Koans

Koan, aforementioned without serious explanation in previous sections, is a Japanese word that means "public dictate." The dictates are meant to awaken your true interior nature. These koans are often essential in recounting the communication between a Zen master and a Zen practitioner, in which the master's question or dictation is meant to reveal the interior meaning of

Zen Philosophy

things in the world.

The earliest example of a koan stems from a Buddha fable. Buddha was said to have held up a flower in front of many different followers. He didn't say anything. All of the followers were quiet and confused except for one of his disciplines, Venerable Kasho. He smiled, recognizing the flower. What was meant to be communicated when the Buddha held up the flower? No one is meant to communicate this understanding via words. Instead, the Zen practitioners are meant to "show" the understanding. Venerable Kasho was showing his understanding by smiling. Confused? It's a deep topic. Essential, koans are a very advanced mechanism. They have no exact power by themselves. However, when they're utilized properly, they can be incredibly enlightening. They are meant to be a sort of can-opener for the mind and the heart.

Koans can only be utilized after you have entered Samadhi, or the condition in which all your thoughts, ideas, feelings, and judgments have fallen away. Your mind is clear and natural. It is free-flowing, and it is allowing you to live in the moment. It is essential to wait to experiment with koans after Samadhi because koans deliberately stir the brain. The Samadhi mind can be stretched, can be taught via the koans. However, the still-thinking, still-confused mind will remain in a confused state if the koans enter it prior to Samadhi.

Koans are meant to be questions or statements that challenge your sense of ego, your sense of self.

Zen Philosophy

KOAN EXAMPLES:

THE FULL CUP OF TEA

A professor filled a practitioner's cup with tea until the cup was full. Afterwards, he continued to pour. The cup was overflowing. The practitioner yelled out: "Stop! It's too full! Nothing else can go into the cup!"

To this, the professor replied: "Life this cup, you are filled to the brim with your own ideas and opinions. How can I give you Zen teachings unless your cup is empty?"

HAND CLAPPING

"What is the sound of one hand clapping?"

BLACKENED-NOSE BUDDHA

A nun was on the search for enlightenment. She made a Buddha statue and placed a golden leaf over it. She carried the Buddha with her everywhere. One day, she moved to a town with many other Buddhas, each with a specific shrine. She wanted to burn her own incense for only her Buddha. Therefore, she built a funnel so that the smoke would yield itself only to her statue. The Buddha's nose blackened and turned especially ugly.

Zen Philosophy

Zen Philosophy

CHAPTER 5. A GUIDE TO GREATER ZEN HAPPINESS

Creating a Zen lifestyle takes a good deal of work—even some work outside of your meditation zone. So many people in the world are on the constant pursuit of happiness. Happiness in our jobs; happiness in our relationships; happiness in our various hobbies. Regardless of where we are in the world, we want to be happy. This is not selfish. It is a natural human initiative.

However, without participation in Zen meditation and exterior Zen attitude, the search for happiness can be on-going. You see, happiness doesn't come after you've achieved specific goals in your life. It doesn't arrive to your house, packaged in a neat bow, the minute you've nailed that new job opportunity or painted your kitchen red. Instead, happiness should be something that we attempt to surround ourselves with at all times. It should follow us in everything we do: from the most mundane around the house tasks to the most incredible, life-long dream missions.

Begin to take action in your life to strive for continual happiness. With the strength of mind you find from you Zen meditation, you can truly find clarity of thoughts to make every action happiness-oriented. You're continually beating back against anxiety, stressors, and depression. Look to the following tips to seize happiness in your daily life. Try to do at least one of the following

33

Zen Philosophy

things every day of the next week, and then re-group with yourself to write down how you feel you've improved.

1. Be Consistently Present.

This is incredibly Zen. When you're living your life, walking through your day, you mustn't think about how great your life will be tomorrow or a year from now. You mustn't think about how great or how awful things were in the past. Instead, you must focus on right now. You must experience every little thing and appreciate the beauty in those things. When you take a bite out of a chicken sandwich, for example, do you taste each and every flavor in the sandwich? Are you appreciating it? Are you noticing the miracle that your body has learned to chew and digest so efficiently? No? Try. Try to practice, noticing each detail as you move forward.

2. Make Personal Connections.

Getting out into the world and creating personal connections with other people is essential to achieve lasting happiness. For one, the connection makes you feel less alone in this world. It makes you understand that you are not the only one with stress, with anxiety, and with depression. It allows you to push forward through your life feeling like you're on a sort of team. Think about it. Some of the worst times in your life were probably times in which you felt utterly alone. You must overcome feelings of loneliness. Do this by:

Zen Philosophy

A) Hugging a loved one. Human touch yields essential hormones in your body, fueling you to feel connected and loved. Human touch is actually one of the best medicines; this is part of the reason massage treatment is recommended.

B) Don't watch as many television shows and movies. When you spend time with your friends and family watching movies, you cannot truly connect with these people. The passivity of the entertainment actually separates you from your people. Instead, look to playing cards, drinking coffee together, or walking outside and talking.

C) Try to listen well when you have human conversations. So many people ignore this essential skill when attempting to make personal connections. People tire of listening to people who can't hear anything they say. These people go on and on without considering the other people's feelings. When you make your human connection, you must listen and ask questions. You must learn to listen by actively engaging and looking at their mouths to engage more than one of your body's senses.

D) You don't have to do it all at once. If you feel overwhelmed by a lot of human interaction, you can start in small doses. Start the interaction in a comfortable location and try to talk about something you know. After you've done a little bit of connecting, you can celebrate this success. When you celebrate, you must remember how good it feels to have that interaction. You can make

Zen Philosophy

small connections and then build on those connections to fuel greater successes.

3. FIND TIME TO SPEND WITH THE PEOPLE YOU LOVE.

This is an extension of the above topic. However, spending essential time with people you love is important in thriving happiness. The people you love are a priority. Cut off your work time; cut off your personal time. Spend time with your family. Set aside sacred moments with these people to ensure ultimate happiness.

4. WORK ON UNDERSTANDING THE THINGS YOU LOVE AND INCORPORATING THOSE THINGS INTO YOUR LIFESTYLE.

During and after your meditation sessions, you will begin to understand yourself and the things you love on a more intimate level. When you understand the things you love, you can understand what activities you want to be a part of your life and what things you don't think are worth your time.

Write down a list of the five activities you love most in your life. These things can be anything from writing to running to painting to simply spending more time outside. Make these things the very foundation of the rest of your day. Try to eliminate everything else (except for work, obviously). It might take you a little bit of time to

Zen Philosophy

eliminate the extra things. For example, you might have to start saying "no" far more often than you're used to. Eventually, the people to whom you must say no will get used to it. They'll accept that you're much happier doing the things you love.

5. FIND POSITIVITY IN EACH DAY.

All people have positive and negative aspects in their lives. Your happiness levels, however, differ based on if you focus on your positive or your negative aspects. Try to alter your mind to think about things differently. For example: if your basketball team lost today, you shouldn't focus on the loss. Instead, think about the time playing basketball as time connecting with your friends and family. Think about the time you were able to spend outside in the sunshine. Focus on the positive aspects of everything. And remember: even the worst things have a positive side. To everything there is a season. We are all on this crazy ride called life. And isn't that a blessing in and of itself?

6. FIND A JOB AND WORK POSITION THAT YOU LIKE.

Remember the list you made earlier, in which you wrote down five things you really love to do. Try to extend this love to your work. If you already love the work you do, then you are lucky—and you should count your blessings. However, if you don't love your work, you

Zen Philosophy

should steer your career into an appropriate place of passion. Even if you're stuck in a job you don't like, you can begin to fuel your efforts toward a different life. You can work yourself out of every bad rut to pursue your dreams. It's never too late.

7. BEGIN TO ASSIST YOUR FELLOW MEN.

There's no greater feeling than assisting others. So often in our lives of separation, we cannot speak to or greet people; we are like separate islands, so far apart. You can push back against this affinity toward separateness and begin to help your fellow men. As the Dalai Lama said: "If you want others to be happy, practice compassion. If you want to be happy, practice compassion."

A) Try volunteering at a local charity. You don't have to volunteer today or tomorrow. You can simply make an appointment for yourself, sometime in the next month, to get out of your house and volunteer in a different environment. You can volunteer at any charity that suits your particular passion.

B) Always be willing to stop and assist. How often have you driven by someone on the highway with a flat tire? How often have you passed by someone who needed help, simply thinking that someone else could do the dirty work? Sometimes, the person who needs help the most just needs a slight assist, like the use of your cell phone or a few minutes of effort.

C) Make yourself available to a sad or depressed person.

Zen Philosophy

So often, these people just need someone who will pay attention to them and listen to their problems. As they vent through their issue, they learn to understand the issue better. As you know from your participation in Zen meditation, understanding the issue—and yourself—is the greatest element to seek true happiness.

D) Take five seconds every day to send a nice email message to someone you love. Toss them a line, telling them how happy you are that they are in your life. Tell them you love them and appreciate them. Just these little words can really help them get through their daily problems and orient themselves in a new day.

E) If your friend has kids, you should offer to babysit for free. You know parents always need a small break from their minions. If this friend doesn't get a chance to get out of the house very often, offer to babysit and set up a specific appointment. This can make a huge difference in your friend's life. He or she won't forget it.

F) Find patience for people who can't understand. Sometimes, people have difficulty doing things right the first time—or the second time, or the third time. Allow yourself to understand their struggles. They are only human, after all. You'll appreciate their patience when you need it.

8. LOOK TO CONTINUE YOUR LEARNING.

Learning is one of the things that sets us apart from the

Zen Philosophy

rest of the world. We can build huge amounts of knowledge in ourselves. We can enrich ourselves, learn about our entire world, and continue to pursue this knowledge. You don't have to go back to school to continue your learning. If you try to learn something new every single day, your happiness will blossom. Go ahead. Google something weird.

9. TRY TO SIMPLIFY YOUR LIFE.

As aforementioned, it's essential to slim your life down to just the basic things you really, really like. As you slow down, you can remind yourself of the beauty of your existence. You can remind yourself just how much you like certain things you used to do, and you can incorporate these things, as well. Furthermore, you can learn to drive more slowly, walk more slowly, eat more slowly, and relieve your stress. Try to stay in the present moment as you maneuver from each thing.

10. LEARN TO EXERCISE.

It can be difficult to start exercising, but belief that exercise is one of the single greatest things you can do to propel your mind to greater happiness. Exercise can help you eliminate stress, boost your metabolism, and lose weight. With this added boost of self-confidence, you can continue to work toward your ultimate goals and reach self-actualization and fulfillment.

If you believe that exercise is too difficult, you need to

Zen Philosophy

decrease the grandness of your current exercise goals. So often, we try to immediately quit eating sweets, immediately stop drinking soda, and immediately run a marathon. Instead, try to make small, easy-to-manage goals. Alternately, if you find yourself without the proper motivation, you need to create the motivation yourself.

Look to the following simple tips to create an essential exercise habit.

A) Write down one simple, easy-to-reach goal. An example of this is just ten minutes of exercise per day. You can increase this goal as you go along. Furthermore, you must be specific about this goal. Ten minutes of running per day? Walking? Weight lifting? Make sure you set your exercise time at the same time every single day to initiate a routine for yourself.

B) Log this activity every single day to motivate you to continue toward your goals. Place the date, the time, and the exercise you did in a particular log every single day. This way, you can look back after a few weeks and see how far you've come!

C) Always tell other people what you've done. Report your daily exercise routine to people in your life. Keep them updated on your specific goals, as well.

D) Remember to fuel yourself with motivation via your Zen meditation practices. Remember who you are and your interior mission. Think of your exercise goals as an

41

Zen Philosophy

essential part to achieve your overall mission toward sustainability and happiness.

Zen Philosophy

Chapter 6. Achieve Enlightenment: A Look Toward A Zen Future

When you reach toward the realms of Zen meditation to feel ultimately fulfilled, you reap all the rewards of mindfulness, of vitality, and of understanding of your own, interior self.

Mindfulness is an eternal acceptance of your thoughts in the present moment. It allows you to exhibit your feelings and actions in real time without giving any thought to bad actions in the past nor hopes for the future.

Furthermore, with Zen meditation, you can eliminate stressors, understand the interior workings of your body, feel a close spirituality with your God, and fuel yourself with better communication. You can feel a part of both the inner workings of your environment and the inner workings of your own self.

Meditation can bring fulfillment to the life of anyone, regardless of your busyness, your flexibility, and your current ability to calm your racing thoughts.

Look to the following lasting benefits of practicing Zen Meditation, and fall into your Zen future.

1. Decrease your bodily pain.

Zen Philosophy

According to a recent study, people who meditate experience less pain perception. This means that they might have greater interior trouble without experiencing as much pain. Furthermore, they report that pain is less unpleasant than other people.

2. CREATE A DYNAMIC SEX LIFE.

When you create interior mindfulness via your Zen philosophy, you can maximize your sex life. When you understand how to live in the moment, you can enhance your sexual experience. So often, lack of self-confidence gets in the way of your sexy time. Build your self-confidence and annihilate your unfortunate inner dialogue.

3. FALL OUT OF CONSTANT TRAPS.

So often, people get caught doing the same mistakes over and over again. When you reap the rewards of Zen mindfulness, you can annihilate these traps. You can let go of bad habits and look toward fresh, better actions to maximize your future. Therefore, if you find yourself always falling out of your diet and losing track of your exercise plan, Zen meditation will help you stay on track.

4. KEEP CALM AND REGULATE YOUR EMOTIONS.

Zen Philosophy

Do you ever feel like you're a slave to your emotions? Kindness and compassion can be yours in future years with Zen meditation as your guide. Meditation can gear your love and kindness toward your friends and family. It can further help you exhibit empathy towards strangers and help you live a more fulfilling life, full of volunteer work and service. After all: our purpose is to come together, as separate people, toward a common goal. With greater meditation abilities, we can truly strive toward our common purpose and create a better, more fruitful earth.

Zen Philosophy

ABOUT THE AUTHOR

My mission with this is to be able to help inspire and change the world, one reader at a time.

I want to provide the most amazing life tools that anyone can apply into their lives. It doesn't matter whether you have hit rock bottom in your life or your life is amazing and you want to keep taking it to another level.

If you are like me, then you are probably looking to become the best version of yourself. You are likely not to settle for an okay life. You want to live an extraordinary life. Not only to be filled within but also to contribute to society.

Sign up to our newsletter and you will receive notifications on new releases, free books, and special reports just for you.

Click here for updates and free book notification.

Zen Philosophy

ALL RIGHTS RESERVED. This book contains material protected under International and Federal Copyright Laws and Treaties. Any unauthorized reprint or use of this material is prohibited. No part of this book may be reproduced or transmitted in any form or by any means, electronic or mechanical, including photocopying, recording, or by any information storage and retrieval system without express written permission from the author / publisher.

Any unauthorized broadcasting; public performance, copying or re-recording will constitute an infringement of copyright.

Permission granted to reproduce for personal and educational use only. Commercial copying, hiring, lending is prohibited.

May be used free of charge. Selling without prior written consent prohibited. Obtain permission before redistributing. In all cases this notice must remain intact.

Zen Philosophy

OTHER BOOKS BY NATHAN BELLOW

Positive Psychology: A Practical Guide to Personal Transformation: Motivational Psychology: Gain Confidence in Every Area of Your Life (Applied Psychology)

It doesn't matter where you are at in life. You may have an outstanding life and ready to take it to the next level or you may have hit rock bottom. Regardless of your situation, this book will help you.

This book will help you gain a new mindset about life and will improve your image as well as your perception of your self-worth. This happens through different aspects and circumstances in your life as detailed in a chapter-by-chapter guide that you can read. Later on, you can apply what you learn and make these life lessons your own. With this book, there is no other direction but towards your best self. By this handy personal-development reference, you will be able to comprehensively assess where you are right now and find ways to get to where you want to be in life.

Leadership: Inspiring Others The Way The Legends Do

This is for all the leaders out there who are set to make change. This is also for all those who are leaders in the making. We are going to change things, starting today.

This book is made for people who want a guide on how to discover their leadership traits, and it is made for people

Zen Philosophy

who want to discover what it means to become one. It is also to make readers understand that leadership in itself is a skill that is made up of many other skills. Luckily, it is something that can be learned through process, and this book would show you how.

Reading this book would also make you understand why great leaders of history became leaders. It will also show you how leadership in every part of society is actually part of the humanity's need for such people. Here, you can learn how to bring out the leader in you by assessing the situation, just like how all great leaders did.

Here Are Some Of The Things You'll Learn...

Why You Want to Become A Leader

How to Become the Leader that You Want

Making Decisions As a Leader

How To Win Friends

Bringing the Best in Others

Much, much more!

<u>The Power of Affirmations: Improve The Quality of Your Life By Reprogramming Your Subconscious Mind: Affirmations Book for the Subconscious Mind</u>

You're about to discover how to exponentially improve the quality of Your Life by taking control of your inner voice. Find out how your negative Thinking has kept YOU from living the Life that You Deserve. Researchers have

Zen Philosophy

concluded that those with a Positive Internal Dialogue have Higher rates of Success.

Here Are Some Of The Things You'll Learn...

What Are Positive Affirmations

How Positive Affirmations can Help Transform Your Life

Positive Affirmations for Confidence, Self-Esteem, Relationships, Career, and much more.

How to Make Affirmations a Habit

All The Techniques to Use For The Affirmations To Work For You

Much, much more!

Zen Philosophy

ONE LAST THING...

If you enjoyed this book or found it useful I'd be very grateful if you'd post a short review on Amazon. Your support really does make a difference and I read all the reviews personally so I can get your feedback and make this book even better.

Thanks again for your support!

Printed in Great Britain
by Amazon